A Day With Jesus

at the Carnival of Wonders

Written and Illustrated by
Kate Ranstrom

For Jude, Hannah and Jayce
-With Love

ISBN 9798425145116

"No eye has seen, no ear has heard
no mind has conceived what
God has prepared for those
who love him."

1 Corinthians 2:9 NIV

Welcome to the land of God's wonders!

Let the fun begin.

"Taste and see that the Lord is good."

Psalm 34:8 NIV

Ride the Ferris Wheel with Jesus.

You are a friend of God.

Take a spin on the Carousel.

God loves spending time
with you!

Meet the Lion of Judah.

Visit with God's amazing angels.

Be filled with the joy of the Lord.

Fly through the air on the swings!

"In your presence is fullness of joy…"

"…at your right hand are pleasures forevermore."

Psalm 16:11 ESV

"My presence will go with you, and I will give you rest."

Exodus 33:14 NIV

"If you openly declare that Jesus is Lord and believe in your heart that God raised him from the dead, you will be saved."

Romans 10: 9 NLT

About the Author/Illustrator

Kate Ranstrom has loved creating many forms of art since she was a child and has continued to do so into adulthood. As a mother of three she began painting regularly. She loves combining worship and painting together and will often pray for people while she paints for them. For her art is her ministry.

She created her business "Heaven to Earth Art LLC" which she felt led to do after many dear friends encouraged her to keep painting for Jesus and for others.

Her and her husband and three wonderful children reside in the Kansas City area, along with their two quirky dogs.

You can see more of her work, order a prayer art piece (made just for you), and order prints and cards at her website:

HeaventoEarthArt.net

Made in the USA
Monee, IL
11 April 2023